love is most mad and moonly

photographs by John Pearson
poetry by e.e. cummings

Addison-Wesley Publishing Company

Reading, Massachusetts · Menlo Park, California · London · Amsterdam · Don Mills, Ontario · Sydney

Also by John Pearson   To Be Nobody Else
Kiss the Joy as it Flies
The Sun's Birthday
Begin Sweet World
Magic Doors

Excerpts from the poetry of E.E. Cummings are reprinted by permission of Harcourt Brace Jovanovich, Inc. from his volume COMPLETE POEMS 1913–1962, copyright, 1925, 1931, 1935, 1938, 1939, 1944, 1949, 1950, 1953, 1954, 1959 by E.E. Cummings; copyright 1963, 1966, 1967 by Marion Morehouse Cummings; copyright 1972 by Nancy T. Andrews.

Photo credits: page 10, Ed Brandstetter; page 46, Karen Pearson; pages 48–49, Larry Boulet.

Library of Congress Cataloging in Publication Data

Pearson, John, 1934–
   Love is most mad and moonly.

   1. Photography, Artistic. 2. Love. 3. Pearson,
John, 1934–   I. Cummings, Edward Estlin, 1894–
1962. II. Title.
TR654.P389   779'.092'4   78-15703
ISBN 0-201-05555-4

ISBN 0-201-05555-4
ABCDEFGHIJK-FEAL-798

For Liz, a mad and moonly mandolinist
and Karen, a sane and sunly saxophonist

Thank you . . .

Many people help make a book or any creative work. I especially want to thank my editor, Ann Dilworth and Ray Coffin. They both gave so much energy in helping select both the text and pictures that in a real way they are coauthors. Also I can't count the ways in which my daughter Karen and Liz Lamson have helped and encouraged me and influenced my photography and my life.

I would also like to thank the following people who appear in the book; Susan and Larry Boulet; Sas Colby; Raymond Coffin; Linda Worth; Linda and Hal Bennett; Raine; Terry and Paul Duffy; Bread and Puppet Theater; Nancy Bleiweiss; Jenifer and Jaren Dahlstrom; Billy Lamson; the Atterberry family; Jules Bamberger; Janine Scholtz; Steve Bevitt; Roxanne Orly; Aspasia Nea; Shoshana Praver; Pamela Polland; Donald Luther; Richard Stoltzman; Heidi Barton.

Finally I want to thank everyone at Addison-Wesley, especially Joyce Copland, Pat Hatch, and Catherine Dorin, the designer.

Introduction

Cumming's poetry dances with the lyrical and the satirical—sometimes a tap dance, sometimes a waltz, but always a dance of feeling. He once wrote: ''A poet is somebody who feels and who expresses his feelings through words . . . Almost anybody can learn to think or believe or know, but not a single human being can be taught to feel. Why? Because whenever you think or believe or know, you're a lot of other people: but the moment you feel, you're nobody—but yourself.''

Maybe this is why we are all such true poets as children, as dreamers, and as lovers. The part of us that feels is released and there is an excitement and newness to the dream, the lover, or the world itself.

In art and love energy flows from the same source—the river of feelings. Both are full of frustrations, playfulness, and delight in the unknown.

I hope this book may renew some of those ''mad and moonly'' mysteries for you. It has been a dervish dance for me.

be unto love as rain is unto colour;create
me gradually

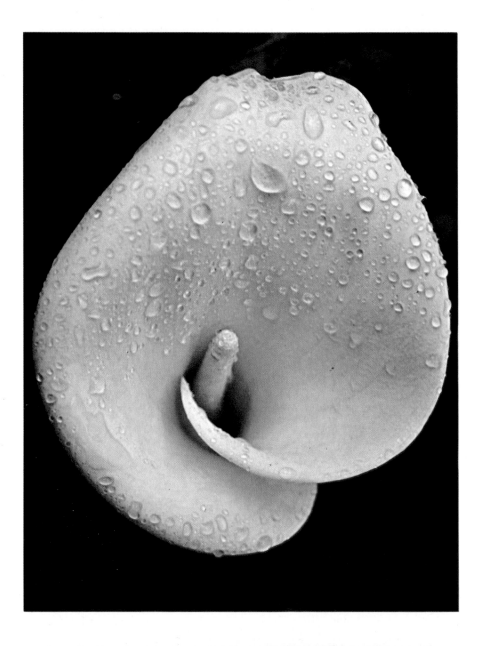

your dancesong
soul.   rarely-beloved
a single star is
uttered, and i

think
        of you

(i do not know what it is about you that closes
and opens;only something in me understands
the voice of your eyes is deeper than all roses)

i like my body when it is with your
body. It is so quite new a thing.

                    i like to feel the spine
of your body and its bones, and the trembling
-firm-smooth ness and which i will
again and again and again
kiss

the holy
city which is your face
your little cheeks the streets
of smiles

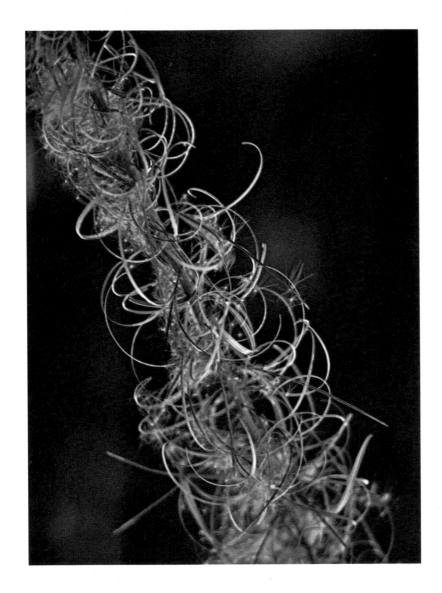

is there a flower(whom
i meet anywhere
able to be and seem
so quite softly as your hair

may i feel said he
(i'll squeal said she
just once said he)
it's fun said she

(tiptop said he
don't stop said she
oh no said he)
go slow said she

you're divine!said he
(you are Mine said she)

it is most mad and moonly
and less it shall unbe
than all the sea which only
is deeper than the sea

it is most sane and sunly
and more it cannot die
than all the sky which only
is higher than the sky

—how fortunate are you and i,whose home
is timelessness:we who have wandered down
from fragrant mountains of eternal now

we're
a mystery which will never happen again,
a miracle which has never happened before—

here's to opening and upward,to leaf and to sap
and to your(in my arms flowering so new)
self

always
        it's
                Spring)and everyone's
in love and flowers pick themselves

and everybody never breathed
quite so many kinds of yes)

there's time for laughing and there's time for crying—
for hoping for despair for peace for longing
—a time for growing and a time for dying:
a night for silence and a day for singing

"sweet spring is your
time is my time is our
time

for springtime is lovetime
and viva sweet love"

lovers go and lovers come
awandering awondering

but any two are perfectly
alone there's nobody else alive

for you are and i am and we are(above
and under all possible worlds)in love

Miracles are to come. With you I leave a
remembrance of miracles . . .

John Pearson

Age 19.
Doing magic tricks at Duke University.

Age 27.
Methodist minister in Napa, California, with daughter Karen, age eighteen months. This was in 1962. (Photo by Josephine Pearson)

Age 30.
Unemployed, divorced, wandering. Begin photography—1965. (Photo by Debbie Ruth)

Age 31.
Trying to transcend the garbage—1966. (Photo by Greg Peterson)

Age 36.
Talking with Anaïs Nin in her home, 1971. (Photo by Liz Lamson)

Now, age 43.
Still looking for the light. (Photo by Lyn Sanny)